FAIRACRES PUBLICATIONS 225

OUR HOME IS IN GOD

John Townroe

© 2025 SLG Press
First edition 2025

FAIRACRES PUBLICATIONS 225

ISBN 978-0-7283-0415-4
Fairacres Publications Series ISSN 0307-1405

SLG Press asserts the right of John Townroe to be identified as the author of this work, in accordance with the Copyright Designs and Patents act, 1988.

All rights reserved. No part of this publication may be reproduced, stored in a retrieval system, or transmitted, in any form or by any means, electronic, mechanical, photocopying, recording or otherwise, without the prior permission of the copyright owner.

The publishers have no control over, or responsibility for, any third-party website referred to in this book. All internet addresses given in this book were correct at the time of going to press. The authors and publisher regret any inconvenience caused if addresses have changed or sites have ceased to exist, but can accept no responsibility for any such changes.

Edited and typeset in Palatino Linotype by Julia Craig-McFeely

Biblical quotations are taken from the New Revised Standard Version of the Bible unless otherwise noted.

SLG Press
Convent of the Incarnation
Fairacres • Oxford
www.slgpress.co.uk

Printed by
Grosvenor Group Ltd, Loughton, Essex

CONTENTS

John Townroe	iii
Acknowledgements	iv
Our Home is in God	1
Christ Lives in Me	6
The Body: the Beginning of the Search?	14
The Emotions: a Hindrance to the Search?	19
The Upward Path of Faith	27
Your God? Your Renewal?	30
Looks like—Glory	39

JOHN TOWNROE

The Revd Canon E. John Townroe (1920–2018) was educated at St John's College, Oxford and Lincoln Theological College. He served four years in a parish in Sunderland before embarking on the training of others for the priesthood. He was first chaplain and then warden to ordinands from King's College London at St Boniface College, Warminster, from 1948 to 1969, before becoming a full time spiritual director, retreat leader and teacher for the remainder of his life. He was elected a Fellow of King's College in 1959. Townroe was extremely highly-regarded as a spiritual director, and much loved. He was also in considerable demand as a lecturer and leader of retreats, particularly retreats for fellow priests, many of whom he had shepherded through their training and continued to support during their ministry.

All of John Townroe's lecture notes and typescripts, some of which were transcripts of recordings, were part of his estate when he died. This book has been collated and edited from a number of lectures preserved in the Townroe archive. Previously published in this series is *Jesus the Undistorted Image of God*, Fairacres Publications 192 (SLG Press, 2022).

Acknowledgements

Because of the age of many of the scripts it was not possible to transfer them into electronic format by scanning. The editors of SLG Press and the executor of John Townroe's intellectual estate particularly wish to acknowledge our indebtedness to Jennifer Potter for the immense task of re-keying so many of Townroe's papers to create digital versions. Without her tireless voluntary work Townroe's words and thoughts could not have reached out to so many and may have been lost to time.

The original location and date of the lecture or retreat is given where known, although not all were marked with the date and place where they were read.

'Our Home is in God': talk to old students at St Stephens, Rochester Road, 30 May 1984.

'Christ Lives in me': typescript dated August 1963.

'Man and God—the Search': Westminster Abbey Advent Lectures I and IV, 1971.

'The Love and Wisdom of God on the Upward Path of Faith': retreat for the class of 1965/66 on forty years in the priesthood, St Boniface Chapel, 9 July 2007.

'Your God? Your Renewal?': talk given at Pusey House during the University Mission, 27 February 1977.

'Looks like—Glory': undated and untitled typescript.

OUR HOME IS IN GOD

Our Home is in God

I want to consider these words from Luke, 'he came to himself' (Luke 15:17) and how they bear upon the present and the future. Our lives contain a wide variety of experience, pastoral, personal, good, bad, happy, unhappy, delightful, painful... Perhaps amongst all this we can recall a time in our lives when we 'came to ourselves', perhaps at a peak moment, and perhaps many times since.

Sometimes others can see it happening—visible evidence, as it were, of the hand of God touching human hearts, and bringing them to Repentance, with signs following. I saw it often in those preparing for ordination, especially in the time leading up to Holy Week and Easter. It could be said, truly, that those were the people whose hearts God had touched. Or, as 1 Samuel puts it, 'these were the valiant ones, whose hearts God had touched' (1 Sam. 10:26).

What does it mean when people come to themselves? We can get at the answer by looking at what it means to be *away* from oneself. To be away from oneself is to be adrift; it is to be alienated from the source of one's being; to be inwardly divided and at odds with oneself. It is the opposite, in traditional language, to being recollected. It is to be out of controlling touch with that deep place within, where we hunger and thirst for goodness, for truth, for God himself above all. In short, it is to be 'off course', for our true centre is in God. If we are 'away from ourselves', what flows in place of that centre? All kinds of falsity, such as acting a part; putting up a show; arranging pretences; things to boost our failing self-esteem; falling victim to fantasy and illusions about ourselves and others; reacting, responding, speaking, never from our genuine depth; using, perhaps, the correct words, but never ringing true.

What do we see when a person (in the Gospels' meaning) is 'coming to himself'? We see, as in the Prodigal Son, someone coming home, someone being drawn to their true centre (as to a centre of gravity), someone undergoing a change of mind, and discovering how to repent. A person comes home, in this sense, by learning how to walk by faith instead of being driven by fear; by finding freedom of spirit through accepting whatever yoke of discipline fits their situation. In this way a person comes not only to themselves, but to God: to a living knowledge of God. St Augustine makes this last point strikingly in his *Confessions*: addressing God, he asks,

> But where was I when I looked for you? You were there before my eyes, but I had deserted even my own self. I could not find myself, much less find you.[1]

Saint Augustine shows how in coming to yourself you come to God and in coming to God, you come to yourself, for our true home is in God. God waits, like the Father who is the central figure in the parable of the Prodigal Son, for the soul to come back to its home with Him. Without that home in God, nothing can have any meaning. Our identity is in God who made us. We become ourselves in God alone. For our home is in God, and it is in being at home with God that we can work out our identity and fulfil it.

Those who, in this way, get in touch with themselves and with God, also get into proper touch with creation, with the created order and material things. They reach a better, more creative relationship with the things they can see, hear, taste, smell and touch. That is to say, their five senses are sharpened and they start to understand their responsibility to the environment as well as to the people around them.

The New English Bible and the New International Version translate the Greek of 'He came to himself' as 'He came to his senses'. If

---

[1] Book V, 2, Augustine, *Confessions*, trans. R. S. Pine-Coffin (Barnes & Noble, 1992), 92.

we press that to its literal meaning we see the implications: we can be 'away from' our senses just as we can be away from ourselves. It is a disease of our civilization to have our senses dulled instead of quickened: the senses are intended to be the means of perception, windows into reality. Instead, here too we may lose touch, quite literally, with a vital part of ourselves and become blind to the needs of our environment and of those around us.

In 1953 a pioneering work of Christian spirituality was published, *My Friends, The Senses*.[2] It was a protest against neurotic spirituality or anxiety-ridden piety, and a pointer to a better way in spirituality and in asceticism to a faith-inspired, positive journey. It was first published in French and had some influence in Europe.[3] Since then, there has been an extraordinary growth of thought, practice and spiritual exercises in the same direction. If anyone today desires to come to themselves and to come to their senses, they might do well to study this literature. However, no methods, no exercise, no religious practice can of itself bring us to ourselves and to God. Methods and practices too easily become dead ends.

How, then, can we come home to God? By Jesus. Jesus is the One whom the Gospels present as constantly living true to the Father, to the source of His being. Jesus is the One who did not keep on 'coming to himself' (as we do), for He was always himself, always 'his own person', as we say, ringing true, manipulated neither by pressures of opinion around Him, nor by neurotic pressures within himself; a man of integrity, a genuine person living centred in God. Jesus, therefore, is in a position to bring us to ourselves.

The Ascension presents to us Jesus returned to His Father's side, His work on earth accomplished. Yet, paradoxically, He is the One who has never been away from the Father: in mind and will, unbroken union with God was at the heart of His ministry. From Him, our ascended Lord comes to us as the spirit of power, the spirit of en-

---

[2] Charles Damien Boulogne, *My Friends, the Senses* (P. J. Kenedy & Sons, 1953).
[3] *Mes amis les sens* (La Colombe, 1950).

abling, so that we too may bring our lives and ministry to completion in unbroken union with God. For what Jesus once did for us, He can now do in us. That is, restore us and bring us home to God.

How wonderfully this can work out in human lives! This was described to me by a priest who had been ordained for about twenty years. He became aware that he was drifting spiritually, and losing touch with God; he was losing heart. He took action by making a retreat, asking God for help very simply and directly—asking, asking from the heart—asking urgently—he cried for help. Help came: he knew afresh the power of God's love working within him, to draw him back to the centre, and to energize his enfeebled will. Altogether, he said, it was 'a bit like coming home'; it was 'peaceful and wonderful'. Nevertheless, although it was 'a bit like coming home', he added with honesty, 'but I still pray to an emptiness most of the time'.

He was indeed given the gift of inward peace, but for him, as for many others, the gift was combined with an awareness of what it was like *not* to be centred or at home in God and a call to persevere anew with a kind of prayer that is stark and bare, and therefore all the more free from illusion, more real.

Our home is in God. Are we coming increasingly to God, as the years pass? Let us ask God, perhaps repeatedly, to keep us down the years, asking for the wonder of His Love which holds us and recalls us and brings us home. But let us also ensure that we keep moving 'homewards', that we stretch ourselves to co-operate with the Divine Love to the utmost of our capacity.

> God is love, and those who abide in love abide in God, and God abides in them. (1 John 4:16)

Steer the ship of my life, good Lord, to your quiet harbour, where I can be safe from the storms of sin and conflict. Show me the course I should take. Renew in me the gift of discernment, so that I can always see the right direction in which I should go. And give me the strength and the courage to choose the right course, even when the sea is rough and the waves are high, knowing that through enduring hardship and danger in your name we shall find our home.

Basil of Caesarea (329–379)

Christ Lives in Me

> I have been crucified with Christ: it is no longer I who live, but Christ who lives in me. (Gal. 2:20).

There is within each of us a turbulent life. Thoughts race through the mind: desires and conflict fight it out against each other; emotions get a hold and shake us with their force. Even the best, even the saintliest, of people will say that what lives in them is often not like a peaceful, ordered garden, but rather like a jungle full of wild, frightened animals and divided by rivers in flood. Not peaceful, but turbulent: not ordered, but chaotic. Under the surface, this is how most people know life, this is what 'lives in them'.

But St Paul says that Christ lives in him: he says it for himself, and he says it for all Christians. In one place (2 Cor. 13:5) he seems to be quite indignant with his fellow Christians for overlooking this fact: 'Do you not realize that Jesus Christ is in you?' he asks, adding one qualification, 'unless indeed you be reprobate'. In some translations this is rendered 'unless, indeed, you fail to meet the test!'—the test of faith. Only that, the critical failure of faith, alters the position. Otherwise, it is true of all Christians that Christ dwells in them. So says St Paul, but many have found it hard to believe him.

Can it really be true that Christ lives in us? Surely not. Surely it is impossible. So there have been various reactions against the idea, such as the attempt to water it down. From the earliest scriptural commentaries there have been readings that suggest St Paul is using figurative language only in these passages: the expressions, it is said, do not mean that the Lord is alive and present in the faithful: they simply mean that the memory of the historic Jesus lives on in us, with the new motives for conduct which He inspired. To hold this view is to make the idea of Christ indwelling much more comfortable and accessible. The idea is brought into line with many other such examples of lingering influence, so the whole idea becomes more manageable, much safer. 'Christ in you' would then be like your other memories or personal impressions: you would know exactly where you were with Him, and would not expect any surprises.

But this watered-down version of 'Christ in You' is not at all what the Gospel offers. According to St Paul, God offers everyone the Risen Christ to be personally with them: what dwells in the faithful is not the image of Christ on earth, but the Lord who was raised up by God. St Paul was not using metaphor when he wrote that, 'Christ lives in me', nor was he referring to an impersonal power felt within him; nor was he referring to new moral energy only.

He meant the *person* of Christ, with all the characteristics of persons, such as unexpectedness, the freedom to do something new. As with all real people, so with Christ in us, we want to be sure what He is going to say next, but we cannot have that assurance. The intimate touch of guidance or of compassion, precisely adapted to each moment's need, this is how the Gospel offers us the indwelling Christ.

Admittedly, it is difficult to conceive how one person can dwell in another. Perhaps it is sometimes for this reason that the doctrine of the indwelling Christ is watered down. How can anyone be 'in' another, separate person? Particularly, how can one person be in another in such a way that there is no fusion of personality, no possession of the other? But rather be in that person in such a way as to make them even more their true self than they were before?

We cannot answer with all the detail we might like, but we can see where the answer lies. It lies in the fact that we are spiritual beings, at least in part, and that Christ who dwells in us is himself spiritual. In the realm of the spirit, there can be an interpenetration of persons, leaving each distinct, but profoundly affecting each, such as is not possible otherwise. Coinherence is the old word for this mutual interpenetration, a word revived by Charles Williams (1886–1945).[4] Coinherence of Christ with the Father and the Holy Spirit; coinherence of Christ and all believers, He in us, we in Him, with the mutual respect of love.

Difficult as this is for us to picture, it is brought nearer to our experience of life in the parallel passage in St Paul where he declares that 'the unbelieving husband is made holy through his wife, and the unbelieving wife is made holy through her husband' (1 Cor. 7:14–16). There is no question here of spatial presence, though we have to think of it spatially. It is a question of spirit teaching spirit and with mutual respect. There is here, in shadowy form, a comparable experience of the mutual indwelling of persons. At the least it can serve to warn us against trying to water down the mysteries of life in order to make them more manageable by the intellect.

Another reaction against the idea of the indwelling Christ is a kind of diffidence or shyness. It afflicts many who might otherwise he ready to accept the truth, mysterious though it is. What prevents them from accepting that Christ is in them, or still more what prevents them from *acting* upon this belief, is a kind of timidity. There seems to them to be something almost indecent in thinking that the Holy One of God, the Ascended Lord, is actually within them. It feels to them like presumption even to entertain such a thought.

This diffidence is, no doubt, a mixture of dread and incredulity, modesty and sensibility. Certainly, it is not altogether bad since it stems from humility, yet its consequences may be as harmful to an

---

[4] Coinherence is the centrepiece to all of Williams's theology; he is widely credited with coining the term, but it was first used in the early eighteenth century. He viewed coinherence as a spiritual principle stemming from the Trinity and extending to other areas of life. The term emerged from his concepts of romantic love, exchange and substitution to denote a universal spiritual principle that worked itself out in the material realm in various ways: things that exist in essential relationship with another, as innate components of the other. He believed that human beings are all ultimately dependent on each other.

individual as the attempt to water down the truth. For this diffidence has the effect of keeping the Christian from entering into the fullness of their inheritance. We cannot realize all the possibilities of Christian living without a certain audacity. It is with boldness that we 'enter the sanctuary by the blood of Jesus' (Heb. 10:19).

Of those of us who are failing to realize in practice the truth of 'Christ in you', probably as many are failing through lack of nerve and a misplaced shyness as are failing by any deliberate dilution or rejection of the truth. None can enter the Kingdom of God that way. We must learn to take it by storm, to knock until the gates open, to be bold in our approach to the throne of grace. Shyness, diffidence, must be overcome, even if it takes a long time.

I have described two main obstacles to grasping the truth that Christ lives in us – one, the intellect's inclination to water down; the other is the misplaced diffidence. But even if these two obstacles to grasping the truth that Christ lives in us were overcome, a much more formidable one would remain unless something were done about it: we may put diffidence aside, and be ready to accept that Christ lives in us, but if the thrust of the ego continues unabated, we can nullify the life of Christ within us, we can render it ineffective. This claim we make to have the right to dispose of ourselves as we will—this whisper to yourself that your body is your own and you can use it as you will; that your time is your own, and you can use it as you will; that money is your own, and you can use it as you will; this resentment against anything that upsets our plans, that invades our time, that interferes with our friendships—all that makes up the powerful ego-drive that is in each of us.

At root is the urge to rule yourself and acknowledge no other, the urge that Satan uses to manipulate us. It takes on disguises, looks much less dramatic and is much harder to spot when it infiltrates the ordinary stuff of daily life. There it may be detected only in indications such as unwillingness to put yourself out for another person, for a community, church, society or nation—to be inconvenienced for the sake of someone else. In fact, the unwillingness to 'go also the second mile' (Matt. 5:41), which is Jesus's way of describing people who will not give that bit extra that cuts across the ego.

In some people it is not so much the *thrust* as the *clutch* of the ego which is the core of the trouble. That is to say, clinging to what they have: possessively to their friends, self-centredly to their own person, jealously to their reputation. Until they let go, they cannot enter the kingdom of heaven.

This is where the first words of the text with which I opened this chapter are important: 'I have been crucified with Christ'. Whatever else these words mean, they indicate the need for a radical break with what has gone before. A radical break with the former attitude to life is the prerequisite of Christ living in each of us. The ego-thrust must be broken and re-directed. The ego-clutch, the tight-fisted attitude, has to be changed into an open-handed generosity towards God and other people. While this is the work of a lifetime, it is also begun, definitely begun, at some definite, conscious point.

Being crucified with Christ is the stark word-picture for the process. But the process begins at a point in time when the 'nails' are first driven in. If it has not begun, then my old life is intact, and my ego-thrust and clutch are unabated. If it *has* begun, if the initial break has been made, then the mainspring of life is radically altered. The ruling disposition is not what it was; and having been thus crucified with Christ, 'it is no longer I who live, but it is Christ who lives in me'. So we return to the central theme, that Christ lives in each of us, a fact which St Paul attributed in the first place to the mystery of holy baptism; but which he plainly taught to depend for its realization upon the conditions I have noted.

So: no watering down, no false diffidence, no shirking of our 'crucifixion'. What more can be done to enter into this experience of Christ within? A great deal more. Divine Grace does not remove the need for effort on our part. On the contrary, it energizes our efforts, and spurs us on to greater efforts, but always it is the effort to *accept*, to *take*, and to *use* whatever God gives.

From within God gives us the ability to worship. Do not put your effort in worship into trying to project out from yourself a perfect offering of praise and adoration, as if you generated these things to be sent out towards Christ yourself. Christ is in you. He is there, already worshipping the Father. There is unceasing worship going on within your heart. Put your effort, therefore into accepting this and using it. Join yourself in the Spirit with Christ within you, energetically. In the Spirit get to that place within where you stand with Christ, and worship *with* Him.

Let us consider the demand that life makes upon us to live bravely. Each of us needs to tackle with courage the evils we come across, in ourselves and in the world around us. Go to Christ who will be within you: put your soul's effort first into keeping close to Him, so that Jesus who challenged the world's evil, who set His face steadfastly, who worked so hard that He fell asleep in a storm-tossed boat, will personally be your courage, your daring.

But there is another direction, especially important, in which the effort can be made to accept Christ within, and that is in suffering. The Christ-in-us is He who suffered under Pontius Pilate and we will never be able to bear our sufferings aright unless we turn to with His presence within us and allow Him to continue His Passion in us. So we must go to Him with an effort and ask Him to bear this suffering within us.

There is a very striking reference to this in Carl Jung's, *Memories, Dreams and Reflections*: Jung writes there about his father, who was a Swiss Evangelical Pastor but an unhappy man, greatly afflicted in soul, burdened with his people's cares, who was always trying to smother his doubts, and never succeeding. 'My Father', wrote Jung,

> had literally lived right up to his death the suffering prefigured and promised by Christ, without ever becoming aware that this was a consequence of the *imitatio Christi*. He regarded his suffering as a personal affliction for which you might ask a doctor's advice; he did not see it as the suffering of the Christian in general. The words

of Galatians 2:20: 'I live, yet not I, but Christ liveth in me,' never penetrated his mind in their full significance, for any thinking about religious matters sent shudders of horror through him.[5]

Pastor Jung never discovered that his sufferings were part of his ministry. He never found the Christ within who was there not to suffer with him, but to enable him to bear it creatively.

*

Worship; courage in tackling life; suffering: These are some directions in which the effort can be made to know Christ within. Practise these directions, and we may begin to realize the possibilities of the Kingdom.

I conclude with a note of warning and a note of joy. First, the note of warning: like Pastor Jung, someone could go all through life and never realize the full significance for themselves of the indwelling Christ. They could work conscientiously, they could try hard to worship, to live bravely, to suffer patiently. But in spite of all this, they might go on keeping Christianity, as a 'thing out there', never fully recognizing Christ as the person within. There is a great divide between these two perceptions, and it is misery to stay on the wrong side of it.

The note of joy is deep, quiet and peaceful because each of us can cross this divide and keep on crossing it. More and more we can find for ourselves the truth of having Christ dwell within us. We can do this because Christ himself enables us: 'search, and you will find' (Matt. 7:7).

---

[5] Carl Jung, *Memories, Dreams and Reflections*, trans. Richard and Clara Winston (Random House Vintage Books, 1965), 215.

Blessed are You, O Lord, who has nourished me from my youth, who gives food to all flesh. Fill my heart with joy and gladness that, always having all sufficiency in all things, I may overflow with every good work in Christ Jesus our Lord. Amen.

St Clement (Pope 92–100 AD)

The Body:
The Beginning of the Search?

What is the Christian attitude to the body, and the part it may play in our search for God? To the Christian, the body is not a thing apart from the real self but is essentially one with it. From the first moment after birth we apprehend life through the body: we receive impressions, and make responses. This is where we begin, you could say, in the body and through the body and this is also where we shall end.

As a child grows and consciousness increases, so does its curiosity. The search is on! Little by little, as more impressions are received, the self grows by responding to all that comes to it and by seeking for more. The child becomes the adult, in whom an inner life has now developed.

In every person there is a drama going on; a more-or-less turbulent inner world of thought, feeling, longing and multiple impressions from the past; within this body there may well be tensions, even conflicts, a struggle, perhaps, between good and evil. Moving along with this body is an immensely complex pattern of relationships with other people, stretching back into the past and reaching out into the present and future. This is a great wonder: a world within a world, located in each human body. It is an everyday marvel so common that we scarcely recognize it. But it is there within everyone.

It was something of this mystery of persons which John Lehman touched upon in a poem written during the last war:

> Soldier I watch so proudly pass,
> Beneath the ruined vault of glass,
> With eyes the desert wind has blown,

> Anonymous, yet always known,
> O, in your look and carriage dwell,
> Mysteries of Heaven and Hell.[6]

'Mysteries of Heaven and Hell' are within each of us, partly revealed by our 'look and carriage' partly hidden. For this, we may reverence the human body—every human body—and stand in awe of the mysteries which it enshrines. But these are mysteries of heaven and hell, of conflict. From this point of view the human body is seen, in a sense, as a battleground, an arena of conflict between good and evil in which the flesh itself, with its many instincts and demands, gets caught up. When taken to an extreme, this view takes the body itself as the enemy: one of the early Christian Fathers of the Desert, the Abbot Daniel, used to say:

> In proportion as the body grows, the soul becomes enfeebled; and the more the body becomes emaciated, the more the soul grows.[7]

I believe such an attitude was formed perhaps more by Greek (Neoplatonist) influence than by the Spirit of Christ. Contempt for the body has always been a deviation from mainstream Christian thought, for if Christ was born of Mary, if God in Christ took flesh for his own, if a real human body was His, if in His Body He searched for us and found us, if He gave himself in love to the world through His body—in life and in death—so consecrating the body for ever—as He said, 'This is my Body, which is given for you' (Luke 22:19)—then contempt for the human body is out of the question for the Christian. This positive attitude means 'for the love of God control your body and soul alike with great care and keep as fit as you can'.[8]

---

[6] 'In a London Terminus', in John Lehmann, *The Age of the Dragon: Poems, 1930–1951* (Harcourt, Brace, 1952), 104.

[7] E. A. Wallis Budge, trans., *Sayings of the Fathers*, vol. 2 (Chatto & Windus, 1907), 22. Reprinted in 2018 by Christian Classics Publishers.

[8] From *The Cloud of Unknowing*, translated in A. C. Spearing, *The Cloud of Unknowing and Other Works* (Penguin, 1978), 109.

Our bodies, we are told by St Paul, are temples of the Holy Spirit. In other words, God himself dwells within our bodies (1 Cor. 6:19–20). In Christian eyes, it is not so much the body which is the enemy, as the divided will of humanity; people divided against themselves: civil war within. This is the real trouble. We need to master ourselves to become whole, integrated and single-minded. This does come about, gradually, when we acknowledge an authority higher than ourselves, that is, Jesus as Lord. There is, then, a necessary struggle, not against the flesh, but for it, that it may be controlled and well directed.

> I punish my body and enslave it, so that after proclaiming to others I myself should not be disqualified. (1 Cor. 9:27)

That is how St Paul puts it: mysteries of heaven and hell again! In other words, there is such a thing as losing God as well as finding Him, and in both the body plays a vital part.

Another point of view, equally important, sees the body as our link with the earth. We are composed of particles of the earth; we are replenished from the very stuff of the earth, which is taken into ourselves by eating, digestion and metabolism. By this means, we have a union with all creation. We are members one of another, finding God in our search and being found by God; a kinship with all humankind, and a fellowship in substance with the the entirety of the planet and all its diverse creatures. Thus, in us the earth is taken up and changed into fuel for thought, for fine feeling, even for love itself.

'How deeply man is rooted in the universe', wrote the Jesuit scientist, Teilhard de Chardin;

> how unmistakably all preceding life is refashioned in man on a new and higher plane ... to think, we must eat. That blunt statement (depressingly and magnificently obvious) reveals, according to the way we look at it, either the tyranny of matter or its spiritual power.[9]

---

[9] *The Phenomenon of Man* (Collins, 1960), 63, cited in H. de Lubac, *the Religion of Teilhard de Chardin* (Desclée Company, 1967), 81.

We have here another facet of the Christian attitude to the body; the earth is fulfilled, and we in our search are fulfilled in serving spiritual ends; God can be found in yielding our bodies to Him, in action and in suffering; God is found in doing His will on earth, in the affairs of the earth.

From this standpoint (of the union with all creation) we catch a glimpse of a more distant vision. As those of the Eastern Orthodox Church put it, Christ was transfigured in His body, in the days of His flesh, when He yielded himself to the Father's will; and the whole world is also to be transfigured, chaos into cosmos, disorder into beauty, beginning now and completed in the end—when 'God may be all in all' (1 Cor. 15:28).[10] Then we too shall be changed, and with fresh eyes in a new, transfigured body, we shall see God. 'We will see him as he is' (1 John 3:2), says St John with confident hope—'Every eye will see him' (Rev. 1:7)—the search ends there.

Those who would find God must seek with the whole of their being, including the will. This means that we need the willingness to take what God gives, and to give what He asks. The search for God always goes wrong if it becomes an attempt to 'get an experience'—any particular experience—for God is known by faith, not (in this world) by sight. We may or we may not get the spiritual experience we think we should like. But to learn to walk by faith and not by sight is worth more than all the 'experiences' put together. Jesus said:

> Ask, and it will be given you; search, and you will find; knock, and the door will be opened for you. (Matt. 7:7)

Let us ask the Holy Spirit to guide us in our seeking:

> Be still before the Lord, and wait patiently for him. (Ps. 37:7)

---

[10] This paraphrases the statement, 'in all chaos there is a cosmos, in all disorder a secret order, in all caprice a fixed law, for everything that works is grounded on its opposite', from Carl Jung, *The Archetypes and the Collective Unconscious,* trans. Richard Francis Carrington Hull (Princeton University Press, 1969), 32.

Gracious and Holy Father, give us the wisdom to discover You, the intelligence to understand You, the diligence to seek after You, the patience to wait for You, eyes to behold You, a heart to meditate upon You, and a life to proclaim You, through the Spirit of Jesus Christ our Lord.

St Benedict (480–543)

The Emotions: A Hindrance to the Search?

Emotions I take to be simply what a person is feeling and I want to divide them straight away (largely for convenience) into positive and negative. I begin with the positive emotions, such as gladness, delight, pleasure, curiosity, contentment, tenderness, happiness, confidence and, above all, love and joy. Could these ever be a hindrance in the search? Surely not! But anything can be misused, and it does sometimes happen that people who are rich in positive emotions grow complacent and insensitive.

For instance, some religious people who have never had any serious doubts in their lives and who have an untroubled happiness in their religion, can—might—become insensitive to others to whom faith does not come so easily. Affluence of any kind, material or spiritual can make us less aware of those in need, but it need not, and certainly the positive emotions may have the opposite effect, they may help us to see more clearly. Love, for instance, is not blind, as people say. Real love is acutely perceptive. Joy, too, can heighten our perception, as the integrity of delight intensifies our vision.

Emotions of this kind play a part in our vision of God, especially when God gives some new insight, or some deeper assurance. We have, for example, the record of what happened on 23 November 1654 to Blaise Pascal, a record which he wrote down in a few broken words on a scrap of parchment and carried, sewn up in his doublet, for the rest of his life.[11]

---

[11] 'Pascal's Memorial', originally written in a mixture of Latin and French, translated by Kathleen O'Bannon in *Christian Classis Ethereal Library*, https://ccel.org/ccel/pascal/memorial/memorial (accessed 5 Feb 2025).

The year of grace 1654,
Monday, 23 November, feast of St. Clement, pope and martyr, and others in the martyrology.
Vigil of St. Chrysogonus, martyr, and others.
From about half past ten at night until about half past midnight, FIRE.
'GOD of Abraham, GOD of Isaac, GOD of Jacob'
not of the philosophers and of the learned.
Certitude. Certitude. Feeling. Joy. Peace.
GOD of Jesus Christ.
Deum meum et Deum vestrum. [My God and your God.]
'Your GOD will be my God.'
Forgetfulness of the world and of everything, except GOD.
He is only found by the ways taught in the Gospel.
Grandeur of the human soul.
'Righteous Father, the world has not known you, but I have known you.'
Joy, joy, joy, tears of joy.
I have departed from him:
Dereliquerunt me fontem aquae vivae. [They have forsaken me, the fount of living water.]
'My God, will you leave me?'
Let me not be separated from him forever.
'This is eternal life, that they know you, the one true God, and the one that you sent, Jesus Christ.'
Jesus Christ.
Jesus Christ.
I left him; I fled him, renounced, crucified.
Let me never be separated from him.
He is only kept securely by the ways taught in the Gospel:
Renunciation, total and sweet.
Complete submission to Jesus Christ and to my director.
Eternally in joy for a day's exercise on the earth.
    Non obliviscar sermones tuos. [Not to forget your words.] Amen.

This philosopher and scholar was brought to a knowledge of the living God; knowledge which transcended anything he had known before.

Positive emotion of this kind is not experienced in solitude only: equally important and life-changing is the shared emotion when the Church as a body celebrates its faith in God. I am thinking particularly of the Eucharist, when in the breaking of the Bread together the Church has a celebration. The very word, if not so much overladen, would suggest joy: joy that Christ is risen from the dead. This is the mainspring of the Christian's deepest emotion, as it is also the mainspring of the Christian's action. Every good Church service is a sharing in the joy of Easter, it is a communication of joy, not necessarily in a highly demonstrative way. It is often quietly, concealed, but none the less real. A good Liturgy can release people emotionally, help them to express what is deep in their hearts and so lead them into worship. Worship: the place where God finds us, and we find God.

Christ has died! Christ is risen! In Christ shall all be made alive.[12]

But there is another side to the question, and for this we must turn now to the negative emotions. By these, I mean such feelings as sadness, anger, jealousy, fear, resentment, grief, pain, anxiety, despair, digust—not forgetting apathy, or a state of non-feeling, as if under an emotional anaesthetic. Negative emotions can build up into great intensity and become enormously powerful. They can occupy us to the point of obsession and, as springs of action, be tightly coiled indeed. We speak, for instance, of 'seeing red', and the phrase is more than a metaphor: we do see red. The body is caught up in the emotions and our whole perception is filtered through the coloured lens of our anger. Here too, our vision is affected, this time for the worse: seeing, we do not see, if we are blind with rage.

It might be thought, therefore, that negative emotions are simply bad, and sure to be a hindrance in our search for God, but it is not as simple as that. For one thing, if positive emotions can lift us to the heights, negative ones can plunge us into the depths, and the depths are as much a part of reality as the heights. In the depths, we can no

---

[12] Cf. 1 Cor. 15:22.

longer be trivial; the superficial is peeled off, and we are face to face with ourselves as never before. And not only with ourselves but face to face with the common humanity which we share with all people. We are all made of the same stuff: priests, politicians, doctors, soldiers, bankers, social workers, parents, children, thieves, murderers, drug-addicts, alcoholics, terrorists. It may be a shock to us to discover the latent forces within, but it is a step towards reality. Those who gain the knowing of themselves gain the knowing of God, as many Christian writers down the ages have said; the one can lead to the other.

So it was said of the Prodigal Son, in the parable Jesus told, that in the far country, in the depths of poverty and in despair, the Prodigal 'came to himself' (Luke 15:17) — I feel this translation is richer and stronger than the versions that translate the phrase 'he came to his senses'. It was in coming to himself that he was moved to return home: 'I will get up and go to my father...' (Luke 15:18). This is the prize that a negative emotion can bring us. In coming to ourselves, we come to reality; and in coming to reality — to the truth, that is — we come to God.

Our heavenly Father (as in the parable) runs half-way to meet us, and when we reach Him embraces us. In fact, the Father has been with us all along, never deserting us. For the Holy Spirit has been drawing us, drawing us out of despair, into new hope; hope with a depth to it such as never could have been, unless we had been in the depths. My point is not that we should seek the emotions which cast us down, it is that in the search for God we should not oversimplify and make the mistake of thinking that we must merely repel the negative emotions as if they were enemies. They can become our allies if we find a better way of dealing with them.

Negative and positive emotions are related to each other somewhat as tragedy is related to comedy. Both are part of life. We need both to enter into the fullness of living. To run away from the tragic is as wasteful as to ignore the comic. To run away from black emotions is as wasteful as to give no outlet to the joyous, for beneath every violent emotion lies a potential force for good. Beneath jealousy, for example, may lie a capacity for loyalty and single-mindedness. Beneath anger, may lie a capacity for caring. Those vital forces of our nature need to be cultivated; we need to detect them, recognize them for what they are, keep in touch with them, and put them to good use.

Does this mean that we are not to check emotions such as anger or resentment? No, not at all. We must control them if we are not to do great harm to others. Normally, we can, by an effort of will, put a bridle on them and that effort is good for us, for we grow through making it. We grow out of childish bondage, into properly coordinated human beings. In a word, we grow *finer* for the struggle.

However, a serious mistake may be made at this point: people can imagine that to restrain emotion by the exercise of the will means to repress it altogether. It sometimes happens that people are frightened by what they have seen of these strong forces within themselves. They are afraid of what might happen if they were overpowered by them, they might commit some offence and suffer disgrace. So, without exactly thinking what they are doing, they attempt to drive the emotions underground. In effect, they are saying to themselves, 'if I can keep this feeling out of my life, I shall be safe'. This is an understandable reaction, but it is mistaken and only leads to worse trouble in the end. Drive the water of a river underground, and it will re-appear elsewhere; try to bury strong emotion and it will come out again, and catch us unawares, for we would be trying to reject something that is truly part of ourselves, and we cannot do that.

Religious people are sometimes particularly prone to this mistake. Whether they have understood it correctly or not, their religious belief or background may have led them to believe that they ought not only to be good but also to feel good. I mean that they feel the 'right' emotions towards God and their neighbours, such as patience, love, devotion, and so on. Anything else (they are sure) would not be acceptable in the sight of God. Therefore, if they are conscious of a negative emotion stirring within they become anxious and deeply disturbed. They feel guilty and rejected, so they try to reject the passion as if that were the unacceptable thing. They suppose that, freed from passion, they might find God again.

A priest-psychiatrist related a case in point from his experience. A certain woman aged 26 was leading a very correct life, always self-controlled, very devout, and persevering in prayer. But she fell ill of a spiritual sickness. She would wake up at night feeling she had fallen through ice and was in danger of drowning. She sank into a great solitude, in which she experienced her own self as separated from the surrounding world by a thick pane of glass. She continued to live among human beings, but it was as though she had no further contact with them. Instead, her solitude became peopled with gloomy ideas of guilt and depravity; she imagined that God had cast her out. When she slept, devilish dreams disturbed her; in which she was attacked by dreadful animals and was powerless to make any defence. Terrified, she would awake and sit up for hours, fearing to dream again. The result was general exhaustion. She looked for help and comfort in religion, especially in the Bible, but this only made her condition worse.

What was the meaning of this fearful experience? It was an extreme case of what happens if we try to deny nature. The woman had tried to live as if her natural instincts did not exist. By a strong will, she had always been in control of herself, and always reversed the dark 'irrational' feelings whenever they arose. The day had come when the instinctive forces had broken out, like animals from a cage, and attacked her, but she had no defence against them because, in fact, it was a natural part of her own nature which was struggling to emerge.

Those who would find God must accept themselves as they are before they can begin to be changed for the better. To deny our own nature (even the rawest part of it) is tantamount to denying God who made us. It is no use searching for God the Creator, if we are rejecting that part of Creation which is ourselves.

As a first step, then, we must face the raw material of our own nature, and not run away from it. We must face the truth—our own truth. It has been said: 'to live a spiritually healthy life one must find one's own truth, and to find one's own truth, the natural soul must be laid bare.'[13] Next, we must wrestle with the inner forces, to refine and cultivate them. Nature is disordered (or 'fallen', as we say): it is not to be repressed, but it must not be allowed free rein either. It must be wrestled with, so as to incorporate the inner forces with the total life of the soul.

If negative emotions are accepted and turned to good use like this they are not a hindrance in the search for God. For we find God in doing His will; and it is His will that we should work with Him to make a greater glory out of all the materials we have.

I want to end this chapter with a note about apathy—and, if possible, a word of comfort. For if some feelings are very distressing, how much more distressing it can be to feel no emotion at all! How especially distressing it can be, at times like Easter and Christmas, to want to love God and to feel that we do not. There could be many different reasons for this: ill-health, exhaustion, shock, bereavement, sin, God's leading us along the way of faith and trust—all are possibilities, but there is one reason I am constrained to give, for the sake of anyone to whom it might apply: just as some people can be too deeply hurt to be able to show their grief, so people may be too deeply stricken with love for God to be able to show it demonstratively even to themselves, so deep is the yearning. It is, as it were, the extreme spiritual form of not wearing their hearts on their sleeves. They can be assured that all is well, but they have this burden to carry. To them, as to all of us in our search for God, Jesus says:

> Come to me, all you that are weary and are carrying heavy burdens, and I will give you rest. (Matt. 11:28)

---

[13] Josef Goldbrunner, *Holiness is Wholeness* (Pantheon, 1955), 31.

O Lord, who hast mercy upon all, take away from me my sins, and mercifully kindle in me the fire of thy Holy Spirit. Take away from me the heart of stone, and give me a heart of flesh, a heart to love and adore thee, a heart to delight in thee, to follow and to enjoy thee, for Christ's sake.

St Ambrose (c. 339–397)

The Upward Path of Faith

This title refers to a common experience along the way of faith, which usually comes in the second half of life. This is not easily described. I need an image to help me to express it. I shall choose the image of a journey up a mountain.

The journey begins, let us say, low down in a green valley amid houses and churches and familiar landmarks. The path is clearly marked and well trodden. The path begins to go upwards and to become less clearly defined. The going gets tougher: fewer signposts, stones become rocks, mists appear, the view fades. And then the path itself becomes obscure, the landmarks quite gone, and there is less and less to steer by. Then the visibility drops to nil, clouds descend, the scene grows dark and the climber feels lost. And then at last—quite suddenly—the clouds part, light blazes, and the climber has a view more glorious than they have ever seen before. Such can be the experience of one who dares to climb a mountain. This will surely recall the journey described in Dante's *Divine Comedy*. Such may be the spiritual experience, point by point, of anyone who dares to follow the calling of God.

In answering the call, the path may begin in the green valley of fresh ideas, fresh insights, fresh stirrings in the heart. Often, too, there is an exhilarating vision for the future. The path of discipleship is marked out, the route is well-defined and well-trodden. Then the path becomes steeper and the going gets tougher: discipleship throws up difficulties in daily life; problems may arise in personal or family life. The fresh air of the initial inspiration can be lost. Staleness can replace freshness. Worse still, for many the familiar landmarks of faith may fade and the points of spiritual reference look suddenly less certain.

This is when some cry out in hurt complaint, 'But the Church is no longer the same Church I was born into!'

Others find that some familiar theological landmarks have disappeared from view and some ethical and moral landmarks as well. Even the most faithful disciples can seem to themselves to be in a kind of fog and to feel lost.

The place in which we are most likely to become keenly aware of this is in prayer, for prayer is the focus of life. Prayer is the focus of consciousness directed towards God. Therefore it is prayer that had hitherto been clear and filled with inner light that can become clouded, less clearly defined by words and concepts. In prayer we find a new kind of darkness, but it is in prayer also that something else happens. The disciple who stays with it, who hangs in there in the dark, can find—quite suddenly—that a new, deeper level of relationship with God is given, a union stronger than anything known before. Below the level of words or concepts or mental pictures or moods, is the gift of stability. Here the Lord's meaning in our lives is revealed. It is the love and wisdom of God that draws us on the upward path of faith, liberates us from dependence on familiar landmarks, gently separates us from the things we cling to which, though good for us once, are good for us no longer. We may see with amazement how ingeniously God's grace has led us through the dark times.

Oh, the wisdom, the ingenuity, the inventiveness of the Lord our God who finds the way to draw us so lovingly closer to himself! So my message is the Good News of the Gospel: 'Love is our Lord's meaning'.[14] Go with the flow of what the Lord is doing in your life, precisely in the actual circumstances of the moment. Be open to receive fresh insights. Wait upon God by plenty of stillness and silence every day. Expect new developments.

---

[14] Julian of Norwich, *Revelations of Divine Love*, Chapter 86.

We pray that God will make known to us his love and wisdom
on the upward path of faith in our lives—in whatever form it
may be taking for us at this moment.

J. T.

Your God? Your Renewal?

What is renewal? How does it come about? Do you really want it? Are you ready to pay the price for it? The renewal I refer to is a spiritual one. It is the work of the Holy Spirit in those who are willing to receive it. It is a personal renewal, so it affects the whole person: spirit, mind, body, emotions, the will. It never comes by manipulation from the human side, but always as a gift from God. It is His personal gift to us. The gift of what? The gift of himself; the gift of His life to us. His life which, like a flowing stream, catches us up in its current, redirects our course, and carries us with its strength.

How does renewal come? It comes by an 'exchange' between God's living Spirit and our spirit. God first moves towards us, and calls us by a mighty attraction, the magnet of His love, and so evokes our surrender, the surrender of ourselves to Him. We give ourselves to God. Then, in exchange, God gives himself to us, totally. Cardinal Suenens (1904–1996, a pioneering voice of the Catholic Charismatic Renewal Movement), said that not one drop of Christ's blood was shed for each of us, but Christ poured out all His life-blood, all of himself, for each.[15] This is the beginning of renewal: when Christ's presence makes itself known, when His indwelling presence begins to influence us from within to kindle a new flame of love for God and for all God's children. It begins to implant the new heart and the new Covenant which the prophet Jeremiah spoke of (Jer. 31:31–4), the Law written on the tablets of the heart. In other words, a new desire is implanted, a profound desire for God and for goodness. At last we really

---

[15] Léon Joseph Cardinal Suenens, *Christian Life Day by Day* (Newman Press, 1964), 12.

want goodness, instead of merely trying to keep the rules. We want God, and we want the good, the true and the beautiful; want them from the heart made new.

When I speak of spiritual renewal coming to us by the way of exchange between the living God and ourselves, I am using an old Christian metaphor: 'O wise exchange!' says an ancient hymn.[16] I am drawing too upon the metaphor's development by Charles Williams (1886–1945), the poet, novelist and playwright who once lectured in Pusey House on 'Is there a Christian literature?'. He used this metaphor as a key to unlock many doors; and I should like to use it to illustrate how the way of exchange works out in three human situations.

I will look at this question of how I can be renewed in three ways: firstly from my guilt, and my shameful self, which refers to release from the past; then from my weakness, and my divided self, which refers to coping with the present; and finally from my despair, and my hopeless self, which refers to facing the future.

My Guilt, and my Shameful Self

> Jesus, full of the Holy Spirit, returned from the Jordan and was led by the Spirit in the wilderness, where for forty days he was tempted by the devil. He ate nothing at all during those days, and when they were over, he was famished. The devil said to him, 'If you are the Son of God, command this stone to become a loaf of bread.' Jesus answered him, 'It is written, "One does not live by bread alone."' Then the devil led him up and showed him in an instant all the kingdoms of the world. And the devil said to him, 'To you I will give their glory and all this authority; for it has been given over to me, and I give it to anyone I please. If you, then, will worship me, it will all be yours.' Jesus answered him, 'It is written, "Worship the Lord your God, and

---

[16] William Bright (1824–1901), NEH 189, St Matthew: 'He rose, responsive to the call, / And left his task, his gains, his all. / O wise exchange! With these to part, / And lay up treasure in Thy heart …'.

serve only him."' Then the devil took him to Jerusalem, and placed him on the pinnacle of the temple, saying to him, 'If you are the Son of God, throw yourself down from here, for it is written, "He will command his angels concerning you, to protect you," and "On their hands they will bear you up, so that you will not dash your foot against a stone."' Jesus answered him, 'It is said, "Do not put the Lord your God to the test."' When the devil had finished every test, he departed from him until an opportune time.   (Luke 4:1–13)

Is it not at first our guilt and shame which this episode from St Luke brings home to us? Jesus in the desert faced temptation and overcame it, He did not give in to it. This is a great example to us; but at first sight it hardly looks like good news for us, for it simply highlights the contrast between Christ and us; His integrity over and against our compromises. There were no chinks in His armour; but we know there are chinks in ours. Jesus's victory stands over against our moral failures; failures of which we are rightly ashamed, such as authentic guilt, not of neurotic guilt.

It is possible to detect neurotic guilt by its tendency to see sin where there is no sin, and by the sickness—for neurotic guilt is a symptom of sickness—which cannot accept forgiveness, cannot rest in the peace of God, even after forgiveness has been declared.[17] I am thinking here of genuine guilt, which clouds our lives and hangs heavily upon us when we know that we have sinned; that is, when we have gone against the grain of the universe, against 'the believed pattern of the universe', as Charles Williams called it.[18] We have gone against it by our fault, our own fault, our own most grievous fault. When all excuses have been made, it remains a fact that 'I was the one who did it'. We

---

[17] The Police receive hundreds of false confessions every week, from people who find a momentary relief from confessing, or who may find a perverse pleasure in doing so, and are under compulsion to keep on doing it even when *they are not guilty*.

[18] Charles Williams, *Essential Writings in Spirituality and Theology* (Wipf & Stock, 2016), 12.

must face the truth that we are capable of such deeds, and such failures in love. We need, therefore, to be changed radically; we need forgiveness, reconciliation, healing. We need them all in the roots of our being.

How does Jesus, who withstood temptation in the desert, become not only my great example, but also my friend and saviour? As St Luke said, Jesus 'was led by the Spirit in the wilderness' (Luke 4:1).[19] It was God's plan for the world's salvation that Jesus should take the worst that subtle temptation could do to human nature; should take it, stripped down to bare essentials, as the desert required; should take it, and not succumb to it. The Spirit who led Jesus into this experience led Him out of the other side of it, with His integrity intact. The desert temptation typified and prefigured the rest of Jesus's life and death. Living and dying, He took on himself the worst that evil can do: He took on himself our deterioration, our grief, our inability, evil, and death. In exchange, He gave much more than a great example: He gave His creative power, His joy, His fullness, life and love. Here lies the good news. For what Jesus did for us then in the desert, He can do in us now.

How? On our side, by repentance and confession. There is no avoiding this: we must turn to Christ, have our attitudes changed by Him, *repent*. And, repenting, we must *confess*, in one way or another. We must 'get it out'. This is essential for all disciples. The choice lies in how we do it: alone in private prayer, and/or sacramentally. This decision should not be made according to our likes and dislikes, but by asking the Lord. What does *He* want us to do? This is the question that matters. The decision should be made facing the Lord who said, 'Come to me, all you that are weary and are carrying heavy burdens, and I will give you rest.' Facing the Lord who also said, to His Apostles,

> Peace be with you. ... Receive the Holy Spirit. If you forgive the sins of any, they are forgiven them; if you retain the sins of any, they are retained.   (John 20:21–3)

---

[19] Cf. also Matt. 4:1; Mark 1:12.

In other words, the Lord gives authority to those who are to speak in His name. They have His authority and power (in the New Testament Greek the two words are one and the same) of the Holy Spirit, given by Jesus to His Church, for the comforting of sinners, that we may be reconciled with Christ in His Church, in the fellowship, forgiven and set free. It is facing Jesus as Lord that we should make our decision. I know from experience that sacramental confession, to Christ in His Church, has four special values. First, its corporate nature: after all, my sins have harmed other people, directly or indirectly; and therefore my repentance should reckon with this corporate aspect, represented by the presence of a priest, that is, another human being, and one authorized to represent Christ in His Church.

Second, in practice this way of repentance helps us to be thorough, both in self-examination and in confessing, and to express our penitence. It may be very difficult to put it into words, but it is worth it, because having to put it into words helps us to get it out. Third, it helps us, in practice, to be more open to receive forgiveness, love and freedom. On God's side, there is never *any* doubt about His willingness to give His love completely. But on our side, as in Holy Communion, how deeply do we receive the gift? The point is made, in his own way, by Walter Hilton, the fourteenth century English spiritual writer, in *The Ladder of Perfection*:

> Although forgiveness does not depend principally upon confession, but upon heartfelt contrition and abandonment of sin, I am sure there is many a soul who would never have felt contrition nor abandoned sin, had it not been for confession. For in confession it often comes about that the grace of compunction visits a soul which had never before experienced it but was always cold, dry and insensible.[20]

This is what other writers have called 'the gift of tears', or the moment when, perhaps for the first time in life, someone feels truly sorry for what they have done.

---

[20] Walter Hilton, *Ladder of Perfection*, Book 2, ch. 7, trans. Leo Sherley-Price, Penguin Classics (Penguin, 1957), 124–5.

The Fourth way of confession is *humbling*. This is why we do not like it. We have to stoop low to enter by this gateway. If the centre of sin is pride, then in practice this humbling mode of confession deals a great blow at the heart of sin. Think of the monastic, lying face-down on the floor with arms outstretched in the shape of a cross, confessing before the gathered brethren. Something that most of us will never experience, but there are ways in everyday life of humbling ourselves, particularly by going to the people we have wronged, acknowledging what we have done and the impact it has had, and asking for their forgiveness.

I want to emphasize that confession, however it is done, is not to be reduced to a mechanical transaction, as it sometimes has been, as if you only have to go through the motions, and you are forgiven. No. Confession is a *personal* exchange with Christ in His Church.[21] The way of exchange is like this:

– God by His Spirit moves us to repent.

– We respond, and confess our sins.

– He takes our burden of guilt, and gives us in exchange His presence, loving, forgiving, and releasing.

– We respond again, with our *will*: the will to change course, and to live true to the new insight, and to live a life of love and service.

Thus our guilt, and our shameful selves, are exchanged for His renewing life in us. Forgiveness liberates. It loosens the grip of evil upon us. But evil still has some hold upon us, even after confession and forgiveness. This is my experience because I am weak: I still succumb to evil's attraction, despite the marvellous new counter-attraction of God's love.

---

[21] An engaging description of confession, or spiritual direction, from a layperson's perspective is found in Christine North, *A Kind of Watershed: An Anglican Lay View of Sacramental Confession*, Fairacres Publications 111 (SLG Press, 1990, revised edition 2023).

Weakness and Divided Self

The second situation from which I need to be delivered, and the one that I examined above, is my present one, my weakness, and my divided self. It is here that we can see most clearly that spiritual renewal is a process. It has a beginning in repentance, but all is not accomplished at one stroke. The way of exchange is meant to go on, and to continue indefinitely, for dividedness is at the root of our fallen human condition—the inner conflict of the divided self. This is why we are all, psychologically speaking, more or less 'neurotics'

'For I do not do the good I want, but the evil I do not want is what I do.' (Rom. 7:19) This is how St Paul described his divided self. How can this division be healed in us? Only by repeated exchange with Christ our Lord. He calls us repeatedly to be with Him, to follow Him. We respond, repeatedly, and let go of ourselves, let ourselves go to Him. He accepts us as we are, and in exchange gives us His integrity, which begins to take hold of us. Healing starts with this implanting in our souls of Christ's undividedness, His wholeness.

– Christ's purity begins to cleanse my heart.

– Christ's courage begins to strengthen my will.

– Christ's love begins to warm my coldness.

It is good to admit to ourselves that we have no purity of our own, no courage of our own, no love of our own. The renewing process is a gradual transformation from within, by the operation of the Holy Spirit. 'It is no longer I who live, but it is Christ who lives in me' (Gal. 2:20) is how St Paul spoke of the healing of his divided self. That is, he spoke of a way of union, the mystical union between Christ and His Church in which every member shares, the union which heals and fulfils us as we were meant to be.

It does not follow that temptations cease. The Gospels show that Jesus experienced many other conflicts in His life after that initial desert conflict. The story of that desert experience in Luke ends with a sting in the tail, the words: 'When the devil had finished every test, he departed from him until an opportune time.' Our temptations may not grow less when we repent and begin to be healed; quite the opposite. We may even actually feel them more keenly. This can be very alarming.

Also, the healing-process may sometimes be rapid, sometimes slow, and sometimes seem to have stopped altogether. This can be acutely discouraging. We falter, and fail, and fall. We may seem to be going backward, not forward. Not a pilgrim's progress, but a pilgrim's regress. Then we may get very distressed, and depression may turn into despair, and we may begin to lose hope altogether.

My Despair and my Hopeless Self

This is the third situation from which I may need renewal. Is despair too strong a word in this context? I think not, because it matches reality: it matches our experience of feeling overwhelmed at times by the blows which tragedy deals. It matches the hopelessness we may experience when confronted by evil's rampaging strength, around us and within us. 'Why are you cast down, O my soul,' (Ps. 42:5) the Psalmist cries—cast down as into a pit of despair!

Amazingly, it is the Christian experience that the deepest point of renewal is here. For here is discovered the Cross; the agony; the depths; the burial—and the Resurrection. Jesus, forsaken, touched the depths for love of us. It was from that, the lowest point, that God raised Him. It is, in Christian experience, at that lowest point that we may find Jesus already there, in the depths of our forsakenness and despair; and at that lowest point that we too can be raised from the dead, from the living death of hopelessness. For the Resurrection of Christ is the supreme renewal. Our renewal is our share in His Resurrection, worked in us by the power of the Holy Spirit.

Hope can be given in exchange for despair, *provided that we pretend nothing*. This is the condition of our renewal, that we pretend nothing, and avoid nothing, and come to the Lord as we truly are.

So we must ask ourselves: do we want spiritual renewal? Do *you* really and deeply want it? If you do, then learn this discipline of the spirit, the discipline of presenting yourself to God in whatever state you are, of guilt or weakness or despair, or all three, without any jaunty bravado or defensive pretences. Learn this, the true discipline of the spirit, and God can reach you. Learn to present yourself as you are, and then to wait upon God for Him to act, and He will deal with your past; set you free to cope with the present; and raise you to new hope to face your future; changed by continual exchange.

Father, give us grace to discipline ourselves in obedience to your Spirit; and, as you know our weakness, so may we know your power to save, through Christ our Lord. Amen.

Common Worship: Collect for the first Sunday of Lent

Looks like—Glory

A basic part of our Christian faith is expressed in the words of this beautiful text: 'Christ in you, the hope of glory' (Col. 1:27). This is music in the very wording, in its mystery and in the sounds of the words. But transcending this is the *sense* of the words, and the *assurance* they bring, for here is a double affirmation: 'Christ (is) in you', despite everything, and is 'the hope of glory', despite discouragement about ourselves and the world.

Christ is, in us, the hope of glory. There is assurance in that. This bold doctrine of the indwelling Christ has always for me been the centre of the Christian faith. For it is the link between Jesus of Nazareth then and ourselves now. He is in us, by His Spirit, indwelling even our bodies; and 'in us' in the sense also of being within our experience: he holds the initiative, and makes himself known, and unfolds in the life of each disciple the pattern of His own life, expressed differently in each individual.

From these inward resources we can draw all we need to meet every situation, and from these resources springs our hope, our hope of glory. Of course, it is a peculiar kind of hope. Unique, we may say. Ordinarily, hope is based upon promising signs, as with a pupil, or as when we say we can hope for a good harvest, because the signs of sturdy growth are there in the fields to be seen. But the hope of glory is not quite like that. Jesus Christ died and was buried before He was raised from the dead. And this pattern has always been followed and worked out, wherever in the world the Spirit of the risen Lord has raised people to new life and glory—and not only people, individually, but whole situations—networks of people, churches, communities, parishes.

Always it is by this same strange process, through the Lord's dying and rising, with burial or blackness and annihilation in between; always it is by this process that the glory comes. There are not always promising signs, but we can always look at the worst, and see in it the hope of the best because of what happened to Christ. We can work at the worst in the parish, in our workplace, in our community or wider environment, in ourselves, and at the same time trust that God is at work to bring out the glory.

'When things are dark', Archbishop Ramsey once wrote, 'when life is dead, when human possibilities are exhausted, God acts'.[22] Each rising again of the individual is a glory: that is, a new showing forth of the splendour of God, overcoming our pride and self-centredness with His love, as the landscape in springtime shows a fresh beauty and splendour. You cannot define glory, any more than beauty. When you see it, you know it.

We must be careful here about one point in particular: people, sometimes, are afraid of what I have called 'the worst'. They are afraid to face the worst—the truth—about themselves or their situation, about their community or their family. They are tempted then to gloss over the uncomfortable facts and tempted to pretend that things are better than they really are. We can all do this. But such pretence would prevent the true glory from shining. We should then be left with a fake glory, the glory of our boasting in ourselves, or the showy glory which is a mere facade. It is terrible when people are trapped behind their own facade. No—the way to the true glory lies the way Christ went, by the brave acceptance of the worst, and then waiting for God to act. It was like this that St Paul taught the Colossians to look to Christ to find their hope of glory. It is like this that in a community or group of believers you may see people growing in spirit; when they accept hard lessons and allow God to act in their lives. Like a garden in which seeds are sown, and die, and come up out of the soil with a

---

[22] Arthur Michael Ramsey, Archbishop of Canterbury, *Introducing the Christian Faith* (SCM Press, 1961), 61.

new splendour—a mystery repeated again and again in people's lives. The Glory of God is indeed fully alive in an individual, when human nature begins to be seen in them as it is meant to be: rich, tender, deep, responsive, awake. It begins.

However, a beginning is all that it seems we can make in this life. That is why, when St Paul told the Colossians that Christ was in them as the hope of their glory, he was also looking forward to the future, beyond the death of the body, beyond the end of this world order: away to the life of the world to come and to the glory of the world to come. We are to look forward to the unashamedly better place, and marvels not yet seen. St John said, 'we shall see Him as He is!' (1 John 3:2), of Christ ascended. 'We shall see Him as He is!' Oh, the thrill of that! And the blessed promise of release from any present darkness, and from seeing things only obscurely, as we do now, 'through a glass, darkly' (1 Cor. 13:12 KJV); and oh, what a hope is this, of a better country, where no ugliness of any kind will find a place, and where everything will be radiant with the beauty of God. There is the Hope of Universal Glory.

So then, we are, all of us, only at the beginning. There is more to come, much more. Christ is with us, our home is in Him. He knows what He is doing. He is completely reliable. There is no need for any of us to get anxious, or to put on any show, or try to manipulate our present or our future. We can rest in Him, rest in His indwelling, and learn from Him how we are to go on, step by step. And then at the last, our true glory and the word's true glory will be seen. Our home is in God. There's the wonder of it!

Open my eyes Lord God, that I may see your goodness, your glory, your Love for me.

J. T.

SLG PRESS PUBLICATIONS

FP1	*Prayer and the Life of Reconciliation*	Gilbert Shaw (1969)
FP2	*Aloneness not Loneliness*	Mother Mary Clare SLG (1969)
FP4	*Intercession*	Mother Mary Clare SLG (1969)
FP8	*Prayer: Extracts from the Teaching of Father Gilbert Shaw*	Gilbert Shaw (1973)
FP12	*Learning to Pray*	Mother Mary Clare SLG (1970)
FP15	*Death, the Gateway to Life*	Gilbert Shaw (1971, 3/2024)
FP16	*The Victory of the Cross*	Dumitru Stăniloae (1970, 3/2023)
FP26	*The Message of Saint Seraphim*	Irina Gorainov (1974)
FP28	*Julian of Norwich: Four Studies to Commemorate the Sixth Centenary of the Revelations of Divine Love* Sister Benedicta Ward SLG, Sister Eileen Mary SLG, Sister Mary Paul SLG, A. M. Allchin (1973, 3/2022)	
FP43	*The Power of the Name: The Jesus Prayer in Orthodox Spirituality*	Kallistos Ware (1974)
FP46	*Prayer and Contemplation* and *Distractions are for Healing*	Robert Llewelyn (1975, 2/2024)
FP48	*The Wisdom of the Desert Fathers*	trans. Sister Benedicta Ward SLG (1975)
FP50	*Letters of Saint Antony the Great*	trans. Derwas Chitty (1975, 2/2021)
FP54	*From Loneliness to Solitude*	Roland Walls (1976)
FP55	*Theology and Spirituality*	Andrew Louth (1976, rev. 1978, 3/2024)
FP61	*Kabir: The Way of Love and Paradox*	Sister Rosemary SLG (1977)
FP62	*Anselm of Canterbury: A Monastic Scholar*	Sister Benedicta Ward SLG (1973, 2/2024)
FP67	*Mary and the Mystery of the Incarnation: An Essay on the Mother of God in the Theology of Karl Barth*	Andrew Louth (1977, 2/2024)
FP68	*Trinity and Incarnation in Anglican Tradition*	A. M. Allchin (1977, 2/2024)
FP70	*Facing Depression*	Gonville ffrench-Beytagh (1978, 2/2020)
FP71	*The Single Person*	Philip Welsh (1979)
FP72	*The Letters of Ammonas, Successor of St Antony*	trans. Derwas Chitty, introd. Sebastian Brock (1979, 2/2023)
FP74	*George Herbert, Priest and Poet*	Kenneth Mason (1980)
FP75	*A Study of Wisdom: Three Tracts by the Author of The Cloud of Unknowing*	trans. Clifton Wolters (1980)
FP81	*The Psalms: Prayer Book of the Bible*	Dietrich Bonhoeffer, trans. Sister Isabel SLG (1982, rev. 3/2025)
FP82	*Prayer & Holiness: The Icon of Man Renewed in God*	Dumitru Stăniloae (1982, rev. 2/2023)
FP85	*Walter Hilton: Eight Chapters on Perfection & Angels' Song*	trans. Rosemary Dorward (1983, rev. 3/2024)
FP88	*Creative Suffering*	Iulia de Beausobre (1989)
FP90	*Bringing Forth Christ: Five Feasts of the Child Jesus by St Bonaventure*	trans. Eric Doyle OFM (1984, 3/2024)
FP92	*Gentleness in John of the Cross*	Thomas Kane (1985)
FP94	*Saint Gregory Nazianzen: Selected Poems*	trans. John McGuckin (1986, 2/2024)

FP95	*The World of the Desert Fathers: Stories and Sayings from the Anonymous Series of the Apophthegmata Patrum*	trans. Columba Stewart OSB (1986, 2/2020)
FP104	*Growing Old with God*	Timothy N. Rudd (1988, 2/2020)
FP106	*Julian Reconsidered* Kenneth Leech, Sister Benedicta Ward SLG (1988/ rev. 2/2024)	
FP108	*The Unicorn: Meditations on the Love of God*	Harry Galbraith Miller (1989)
FP109	*The Creativity of Diminishment*	Sister Anke (1990)
FP110	*Called to be Priests*	Hugh Wybrew (1989, updated 2/2024)
FP111	*A Kind of Watershed: An Anglican Lay View of Sacramental Confession* Christine North (1990, updated 2/2022)	
FP116	*Jesus, the Living Lord*	Bishop Michael Ramsey (1992)
FP120	*The Monastic Letters of Saint Athanasius the Great* trans. and introd. Leslie Barnard (1994, 2/2023)	
FP122	*The Hidden Joy*	Sister Jane SLG, ed. Dorothy Sutherland (1994)
FP124	*Prayer of the Heart: An Approach to Silent Prayer and Prayer in the Night* Alexander Ryrie (1995, 3/2020)	
FP126	*Evelyn Underhill, Anglican Mystic: Two Centenary Essays* A. M. Allchin, Bishop Michael Ramsey (1977, rev. 4/2025)	
FP127	*Apostolate and the Mirrors of Paradox* Sydney Evans, ed. Andrew Linzey & Brian Horne (1996)	
FP128	*The Wisdom of Saint Isaac the Syrian*	Sebastian Brock (1997)
FP129	*Saint Thérèse of Lisieux: Her Relevance for Today*	Sister Eileen Mary SLG (1997)
FP130	*Expectations: Five Addresses for Those Beginning Ministry* Sister Edmée SLG (1997, 2/2024)	
FP131	*Scenes from Animal Life: Fables for the Enneagram Types* Waltraud Kirschke, trans. Sister Isabel SLG (1998)	
FP132	*Praying the Word of God: The Use of Lectio Divina*	Charles Dumont OCSO (1999)
FP133	*Love Unknown: Meditations on the Death and Resurrection of Jesus* John Barton (1999, 2/2024)	
FP134	*The Hidden Way of Love: Jean-Pierre de Caussade's Spirituality of Abandonment* Barry Conaway (1999, 2/2025)	
FP135	*Shepherd and Servant: The Spiritual Theology of Saint Dunstan*	Douglas Dales (2000)
FP137	*Pilgrimage of the Heart*	Sister Benedicta Ward SLG (2001)
FP138	*Mixed Life* Walter Hilton, trans. Rosemary Dorward (2001, enlarged rev. 3/2024)	
FP139	*In the Footsteps of the Lord: The Teaching of Abba Isaiah of Scetis* John Chryssavgis, Luke Penkett (2001, 2/2023)	
FP140	*A Great Joy: Reflections on the Meaning of Christmas*	Kenneth Mason (2001)
FP141	*Bede and the Psalter*	Sister Benedicta Ward SLG (2002, 2/2024)
FP142	*Abhishiktananda: A Memoir of Dom Henri Le Saux* Murray Rogers, David Barton (2003)	
FP143	*Friendship in God: The Encounter of Evelyn Underhill & Sorella Maria of Campello* A. M. Allchin (2003, rev. 2/2025)	
FP144	*Christian Imagination in Poetry and Polity: Some Anglican Voices from Temple to Herbert* Bishop Rowan Williams (2004)	
FP145	*The Reflections of Abba Zosimas: Monk of the Palestinian Desert* trans. and introd. John Chryssavgis (2005, 3/2022)	
FP146	*The Gift of Theology: The Trinitarian Vision of Ann Griffiths and Elizabeth of Dijon* A. M. Allchin (2005)	
FP147	*Sacrifice and Spirit*	Bishop Michael Ramsey (2005)
FP148	*Saint John Cassian on Prayer*	trans. A. M. Casiday (2006, 2/2024)
FP149	*Hymns of Saint Ephrem the Syrian*	trans. Mary Hansbury (2006, 2/2024)

FP150 *Suffering: Why All this Suffering? What Do I Do about It?*
                    Reinhard Körner OCD, trans. Sister Avis Mary SLG (2006)
FP151 *A True Easter: The Synod of Whitby 664 AD* Sister Benedicta Ward SLG (2007, 2/2023)
FP152 *Prayer as Self-Offering*   Alexander Ryrie (2007)
FP153 *From Perfection to the Elixir: How George Herbert Fashioned a Famous Poem*
                                                    Benedick de la Mare (2008, 2/2024)
FP154 *The Jesus Prayer: Gospel Soundings*   Sister Pauline Margaret CHN (2008)
FP155 *Loving God Whatever: Through the Year with Sister Jane* Sister Jane SLG (2006)
FP156 *Prayer and Meditation for a Sleepless Night*
                              SISTERS OF THE LOVE OF GOD (1993, 3/2024)
FP157 *Being There: Caring for the Bereaved*   John Porter (2009)
FP158 *Learn to Be at Peace: The Practice of Stillness* Andrew Norman (2010)
FP159 *From Holy Week to Easter*   George Pattison (2010)
FP160 *Strength in Weakness: The Scandal of the Cross* John W. Rogerson (2010)
FP161 *Augustine Baker: Frontiers of the Spirit*   Victor de Waal (2010, 2/2025)
FP162 *Out of the Depths*
              Gonville ffrench-Beytagh; epilogue Wendy Robinson (1990, 2/2010)
FP163 *God and Darkness: A Carmelite Perspective*
                         Gemma Hinricher OCD, trans. Sister Avis Mary SLG (2010)
FP164 *The Gift of Joy*   Curtis Almquist SSJE (2011)
FP165 *'I Have Called You Friends': Suggestions for the Spiritual Life Based on
        the Farewell Discourses of Jesus*   Reinhard Körner OCD (2012)
FP166 *Leisure*   Mother Mary Clare SLG (2012)
FP167 *Carmelite Ascent: An Introduction to Saint Teresa and Saint John of the Cross*
                                            Mother Mary Clare SLG (1973, rev. 2/2012)
FP168 *Ann Griffiths and Her Writings*   Llewellyn Cumings (2012)
FP169 *The Our Father*   Sister Benedicta Ward SLG (2012)
FP171 *The Spiritual Wisdom of the Syriac Book of Steps* Robert A. Kitchen (2013)
FP172 *The Prayer of Silence*   Alexander Ryrie (2012)
FP173 *On Tour in Byzantium: Excerpts from The Spiritual Meadow of John Moschus*
                                                    Ralph Martin SSM (2013)
FP174 *Monastic Life*   Bonnie Thurston (2016)
FP175 *Shall All Be Well? Reflections for Holy Week* Graham Ward (2015)
FP176 *Solitude and Communion: Papers on the Hermit Life* ed. A. M. Allchin (2015)
FP177 *The Prayers of Jacob of Serugh*   ed. Mary Hansbury (2015)
FP178 *The Monastic Hours of Prayer*   Sister Benedicta Ward SLG (2016)
FP179 *The Desert of the Heart: Daily Readings with the Desert Fathers*
                                         trans. Sister Benedicta Ward SLG (2016)
FP180 *In Company with Christ: Lent, Palm Sunday, Good Friday & Easter to Pentecost*
                                                    Sister Benedicta Ward SLG (2016)
FP181 *Lazarus: Come Out! Reflections on John 11* Bonnie Thurston (2017)
FP182 *Unknowing & Astonishment: Meditations on Faith for the Long Haul*
                                                    Christopher Scott (2018)
FP183 *Pondering, Praying, Preaching: Romans 8*   Bonnie Thurston (2019, 2/2021)
FP184 *Shem'on the Graceful: Discourse on the Solitary Life*
                                       trans. and introd. Mary Hansbury (2020)
FP185 *God Under My Roof: Celtic Songs and Blessings* Esther de Waal (2020)
FP186 *Journeying with the Jesus Prayer*   James F. Wellington (2020)

FP187	Poet of the Word: Re-reading Scripture with Ephraem the Syrian	
		Aelred Partridge OC (2020)
FP188	Identity and Ritual	Alan Griffiths (2021)
FP189	River of the Spirit: The Spirituality of Simon Barrington-Ward	Andy Lord (2021)
FP190	Prayer and the Struggle against Evil	John Barton, Daniel Lloyd, James Ramsay, Alexander Ryrie (2021)
FP191	Dante's Spiritual Journey: A Reading of the Divine Comedy	Tony Dickinson (2021)
FP192	Jesus the Undistorted Image of God	John Townroe (2022)
FP193	Our Deepest Desire: Prayer, Fasting & Almsgiving in the Writings of Saint Augustine of Hippo	Sister Susan SLG (2022)
FP194	Lent with George Herbert	Tony Dickinson (2022)
FP195	Four Ways to the Cross	Tony Dickinson (2022)
FP196	Anselm of Canterbury, Teacher of Prayer	Sister Benedicta Ward SLG (2022)
FP197	With One Heart and Mind: Prayers out of Stillness	Anthony Kemp (2023)
FP198	Sayings of the Urban Fathers & Mothers	James Ashdown (2023)
FP199	Doors	Sister Raphael SLG (2023)
FP200	Monastic Vocation SISTERS OF THE LOVE OF GOD, Bishop Rowan Williams (2021)	
FP201	An Ecology of the Heart: Faith Through the Climate Crisis	Duncan Forbes (2023)
FP202	'In the image of the Image': Gregory of Nyssa's Opposition to Slavery	
		Adam Couchman (2023)
FP203	Gregory of Nyssa and the Sins of Asia Minor	Jonathan Farrugia (2023)
FP204	Discovery	Arthur Bell (2023)
FP205	Living Healing: the Spirituality of Leanne Payne	Andy Lord (2023)
FP206	Still Listening: Sowing the Seeds of the Jesus Prayer	Bruce Batstone CJN (2023)
FP207	Julian of Norwich: Four Essays to Commemorate 650 Years of the Revelations of Divine Love	Bishop Graham Usher, Father Colin CSWG, Sister Elizabeth Ruth Obbard OC, Mother Hilary Crupi OJN (2023)
FP208	TIME	Dumitru Stăniloae, Kallistos Ware (2023)
FP209	Pearls of Life: A Lifebelt for the Spirit	Tony Dickinson (2024)
FP210	The Way and the Truth and the Life: An Exploration by a Follower of the Way	
		James Ramsay (2024)
FP211	Cosmos, Crisis & Christ: Essays of Wendy Robinson	Wendy Robinson (2024)
FP212	Towards a Theology of Psychotherapy: The Spirituality of Wendy Robinson	
		Andrew Louth (2024)
FP213	Immersed in God and the World: Living Priestly Ministry	Andy Lord (2024)
FP214	The Road to Emmaus: A Sculptor's Journey through Time	Rodney Munday (2024)
FP215	Prayer Too Deep for Words	Sister Edmée SLG (2024)
FP216	The Prayers of St Isaac of Nineveh	Sebastian Brock (2024)
FP217	Two Medieval English Saints: Cuthbert and Alban	Sister Benedicta Ward SLG (2024)
FP218	Encountering the Depths	Mother Mary Clare SLG (1981, rev. 3/2024)
FP219	Conflict and Concord Sister Susan SLG, Bishop Humphrey Southern, Bronwen Neil, Sister Rosemary SLG, Sister Clare-Louise SLG (2024)	
FP220	Divine Love in the Song of Songs	Sister Edmée SLG (2024)
FP221	Zeal for the Faith: An Introduction to Christian-Muslim Dialogue	Tony Dickinson (2024)
FP222	Bernard & Abelard	Sister Edmée SLG (2024)
FP223	Eliot's Transitions: T. S. Eliot's Search for Identity and the Society of the Sacred Mission at Kelham Hall	Vincent Strudwick (2024)
FP224	Landscape, Soul and Spirit: Ecology, Prayer and Robert Macfarlane	Andy Lord (2025)
FP225	Our Home is in God	John Townroe (2025)

Contemplative Poetry Series

CP1	*Amado Nervo: Poems of Faith and Doubt*	trans. John Gallas (2021)
CP2	*Anglo-Saxon Poets: The High Roof of Heaven*	trans. John Gallas (2021)
CP3	*Middle English Poets: Where Grace Grows Ever Green*	ed. John Gallas (2021)
CP4	*The Voice inside Our Home: Selected Poems*	Edward Clarke (2022)
CP5	*Women & God: Drops in the Sea of Time*	trans. and ed. John Gallas (2022)
CP6	*Gabrielle de Coignard & Vittoria Colonna: Fly Not Too High*	trans. John Gallas (2022)
CP7	*Chancing on Sanctity: Selected Poems*	James Ramsay (2022)
CP8	*Gabriela Mistral: This Far Place*	trans. John Gallas (2023)
CP9	*Henry Vaughan & George Herbert: Divine Themes and Celestial Praise*	ed. Edward Clarke (2023)
CP10	*Love Will Come with Fire: Anthology*	Sisters of the Love of God (2023)
CP11	*Touchpapers: Anthology*	coll. and trans. John Gallas (2023)
CP12	*Seasons of my Soul: Selected Poems*	Clare McKerron (2023)
CP13	*Reinhard Sorge: Take Flight to God*	trans. John Gallas (2024)
CP14	*Embertide: Encountering Saint Frideswide*	Romola Parish (2024)
CP15	*Thomas Campion: Made All of Light*	ed. and introd. Julia Craig-McFeely (2024)
CP16	*When God Hides: Selected Poems*	Joseph Evans (2025)

Vestry Guides

VG1	*The Visiting Minister: How to Welcome Visiting Clergy to Your Church*	Paul Monk (2021)
VG2	*Help! No Minister! or Please Take the Service*	Paul Monk (2022)
VG3	*The Liturgy of the Eucharist: An Introductory Guide*	Paul Monk (2024)

www.slgpress.co.uk

The Sisters of the Love of God is an Anglican community of women religious living a contemplative monastic life.

To learn more about the Community and the Convent of the Incarnation at Fairacres, Oxford, see our website www.slg.org.uk.

As well as supporting those seeking to follow a vocation to the monastic life, the Community has a number of forms of association for those who feel drawn to share in the Sisters' life of prayer: Fellowship of the Love of God, Companions, Priests Associate or Oblate Sisters.

For more information email sisters@slg.org.uk or write to The Reverend Mother, Convent of the Incarnation, Parker Street, Oxford, OX4 1TB, UK.